MOONSPEAK ~ INDIGO
TIDES

MOONSPEAK ~ INDIGO TIDES

TIANNA GODSEY

MoonSpeak: Indigo Tides
Copyright © 2024 by Tianna Godsey

Cover: Tianna Godsey; background image: Unsplash, Benjamin Voros

First printing, December 2024
Second printing, January 2026

Wolf Rose Press: *an imprint*
Birdsboro, Pennsylvania
USA

Hardcover ISBN 978-1-952050-09-1
Paperback ISBN 978-1-952050-08-4
eBook ISBN 978-1-952050-10-7

creativetianna.com/books

All rights reserved. No part of this book may be reproduced in any manner whatsoever without written permission except in the case of brief quotations embodied in critical articles and reviews.

*to all that is,
all that was,
& all that will be.*

*dedicated to the roots & ripples
that bind us to the universe,
and the hearts we carry
along the journey.*

Contents

Dedication	v
Notes	xiii
Chapter	xv

I	WOLF MOON	1
II	WORM MOON	30
III	FLOWER MOON	58
IV	BUCK MOON	84
V	HARVEST MOON	111

about the poet   136

Poems & Prose

I.
WOLF MOON

recherché
morning mantra meditation
w o l f w o m a n (h o o d)
coyote season
3:00am ~ witching hour
peace lily
kiss of the wild
hyper-vigilance
the wraith (*before-times*)
Mother of Thousands
elephant mountains
52-B
wayfinding / wayfaring
my body is saying
new skin
Selkie
opossum magic
decomposition of a tree
infinity lotus
manifestation
4:00am ~ December
hibernation
icicles on my   [edges]
the foxes
after-notes

the moth // the flame
Dear Winter,

II.
WORM MOON

the whispers of wolves
afterglow
Inchoate Dreams: Rooted
I'll follow
elderberry
melliferous
Ravening
my new gravity
autumnal abundance
tremolo
[dating...] for wolf women
ephemeral
glimmers
l i m b o
cosmos
nautilus
silent forest meditations
ammonite heart
war paint
dreams of mud & fire
Laniakea
stretch marks
Like a River
mulberry

III.
FLOWER MOON

luna moth
(woman) of the woods
soul-patching in paradise
traverse
full moon romp
learning the language of birds
esculent
impetus
heady elevation
sequoia promises // gingko season
meditations of a budding plant mom
summer azure
murmuration
moonspeak
interlude
palimpsest
heartwood
the night I became a nudist
dragon-toothed
my Perseids man
dark & stormy: *a symphony*
the muse
a new way of living
after the storm

IV.
BUCK MOON

the caterpillar
(vernal) marshlands
wild terrains
I am learning what home feels like.
giants of the forest
g h o s t   f e r n
desert thunderstorm
I am one with my pack & my pack is one with me
unFURling like a fiddlehead
anamnesis
wolf fangs
signs of self-reliance
The Wolf Queen
dream-quaking
breathing underwater
the way of water
Blue Lake
the snail
wolf den ((building a home))
effulgence
a study in imperfection
indigo tides

V.
HARVEST MOON

tap root
I am blossoming
myrmecochory
the slow burn

reminiscences
entwined (the entanglement)
(scent)-iments
alluvial fan
hiking alone (a woman in the woods)
deliquesce
the meeting: *a love story*
moments I want to remember
i dreamt
the oak & his lichen ~
everyday affirmations

POET'S NOTE

MoonSpeak: Indigo Tides

This collection has been in the making since I first published my debut *Singing through my Wolf Bones* two years ago. It was nothing but a thought, a seed planted in my mind, at that time—and I knew it would evolve as organically and authentically as necessary. The creative process (& our healing journey) is one of many twists and turns, winding serpentine passages—and it never quite leads the way we expect.

Two years ago, I was in a much different stage/phase of my life; as I continued to grow and learn myself, I knew I was outgrowing that version of me. In many ways, publishing my first collection fortified my self-love and healing journey on the path I've found. All the while, my wild Wolf Spirit ran alongside me, guiding me home.

I left what I had come to know as my home, my heart, my beloved—and forged out to create something new. No matter how much it hurt, no matter how much it terrified me, I knew it was the only choice. The act of leaving your own comfort (for me, I found this "comfort" was not actually comfort at all, but a cage), is one of complete courage. Shedding all you once defined yourself as and journeying out to discover who you want to be.

This collection you hold in your hands is one exploring transitions: of the seasons, of life, of our emotions, our healing, our relationships, our dreams, and all the ways these shift—becoming reawakened, dying and being reborn while still living in this body, our whole essence.

The tides of life, of our emotions, ebb and flow—they move in and out, they come to save us and sweep us back where we belong. So journey with me now, on these Indigo Tides while we converse with the Moon.

Stay wild, pack mates.

Wildly yours,
Tianna

XIV -

also by

Tianna Godsey

~ poetry & prose collections ~

Singing through my Wolf Bones

(2022)

Untrammeled: golden-cracked words

(2026)

praise for Tianna Godsey's work

"Within the body of each poem, Tianna articulates the theme of a woman at her lowest, channeling her inner wolf spirit to rise again.

And within those themes, each poem recounts a different saga, a different phase of highs and lows, all the while inching closer to reclamation and freedom of authenticity."

— *Neel Trivedi*

I

WOLF MOON

recherché

        (adj.; rare, exotic, obscure)

this freedom of soul & sprit I have come to know
after many years of entrapment, (encaged by
others' expectations / beliefs of who I was),

I now define my own path, dance to the beat
of my own rhythm. the drums echo deep
in my soul, strumming through my nerves

    thumping on my bones.

I am destined for this freedom, this glory
of taking my life in the palms of my own hands.
discovering just how beautiful it is

to be alive, to share and nourish.
to connect, find love, passion and pleasure
waiting on the other side... unleash

the chains which bound me; unleash
those chains which bind me, still....

    I am free.
        I am me.
            I am whole.

morning mantra meditation

in this moment, I don't have to *do* or *be* anything.
I am the water rushing across the stones, wearing
them to smooth touch. I am the sunshine dappling
through the trees. I am the stones waiting along the
creek-bed to be discovered by the sun and water. the
leaves fallen from their branches to fodder new growth,
the brilliant birdsong swaying on a gentle wind. I am
all that is and ever was—all that will be. the hawk
soaring overhead. the footsteps of another along
the path; the groan of engines digging up the quarry.

I am the rhythm and flow of the Universe;
all things and no-thing at once.

wolf woman(hood)

it's our nature, to be set free.
after a while, the (wrong) things you love
can become chains—   even comfort
becomes a cage.   *you don't realize it,*
at first...   but after a few full Moons
when you neglect to shift,   when you
don't give in to your Wolf form, you begin
to lose a part of yourself.   *until you don't*
even know who you are anymore   —and the only
     way to find   the answer
is to forsake those comfortable bonds...

    to race into the wild
    with that [*human*] skin
    peeled clean off, your fur
    flying free in the wind.

coyote season

the day after I left my ex-husband for good, it was coyote season. I guess you could say, every season is coyote season. sometimes you don't see them at all but they're still there. as we passed by an open field, dry stalks stark in the winter air, I saw a tawny, gray-coated coyote standing in the middle of the field, watching. he was alone, observing. our eyes seemed to meet, like our souls acknowledged each other. my coyote: a symbol of cunning, cleverness, and resilience. of death and rebirth; a reminder that no matter how painful this transition, it was a storm brewing within for so long, a chaos that needed untethering, unleashing. if I must shed what I deeply love to find inner peace and joy, I bare my soul in this vulnerable moment of the complete unknown. I know I will find my feet again; I know great love still exists to be discovered. and now, I cultivate safety and space to breathe. unwinding, unraveling, letting my guard down. releasing my hypervigilance of tension before the next storm, when all I wanted was to dance among the raindrops, feel them on my bare skin as I tilt my head up and laugh into the rain.

3:00am - witching hour

I am withstanding the pain
unlocking my full potential
      reignited with soul-fire.

I am learning to soar again
there's nothing to which I can't aspire
be kind, dear heart; marvelous creature

I am ascendant

purge of the soil(soul)-dredges
digging up murk like archaeological finds.

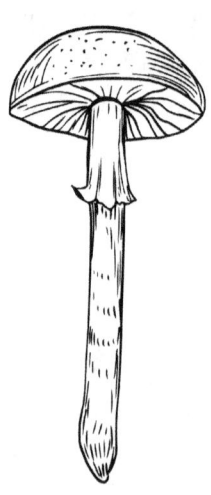

peace lily

a lone wolf
hops from her bath
along the run-off stream
water flows over rocks
a steady rhythm & joy
the trickle of promises,
more wishes to be made
& discoveries deep in dark
crevices. journey beside
the dark wolf and you'll see
beyond her pelt; the glimmers
of love in her eyes, the
seductive flicker of a tongue
over lips. a mo(u)rning ritual
as delicate & sure as birdsong...

kiss of the wild

> *I am no mother,*
> *I am no bride;*
> *I am King.*
>
> — *Florence & the Machine*

I release the need to love someone
who cannot love me the way I need,
desire, and deserve. I release the old
ways I used to believe love should be
and open up new avenues of my heart.
I allow flow, connection, and grounding.
I allow healing. I allow Release. to let go
and welcome in the new, without guilt
or stress or worry.

hyper-vigilance

for many moonlit nights after I decided
to leave him, my heart remained coiled
like a cobra in the seat of my (rose)hips,
a mountain range arched along my spine
and the wild crane of my neck, always
watching, waiting, ready for his return
within the darkest shadows.

the wraith   (*before-times*)

floating through rooms, I don't leave the house
except to get the mail, walk the yard, water flowers.
my hair hangs long, tangled strands unwashed.
the scent of me lingers likes a cloud following
behind. *there is no respite, when I'm the one haunting myself.*
in every mirror, a pallid reflection—every corner, a shadow
of whom I once was, gazing through me like a third eye.
the selves I used to be won't leave, they beckon me to stay
their fingers like wisps of fog hovering around me,
a past I can never return to… a self I must deny.

Mother of Thousands

I've entered a state of deep compression
like a seed huddled in on itself waiting to sprout
I've held tight to my words, my wounds, my thoughts,
my emotions as I enter this new stage
of healing. reintegrating my body/mind/soul
back to feel the earthen roots of my toes
golden threads of my hair like moon strands
I enter a new realm of being, of beauty, of
becoming. and I don't look back except to mark

> how far I've come,
> how tall I've grown.

elephant mountains

part of me will always be that girl
who raced through forests of cacti
straight into the prickly thorns
my father carried me home
my mother picked the cacti thorns
one   by   one
from my skin

my innocence was planted in the
shadow of those mountains
they looked like a family of elephants
leaning against each other, ears &
trunks wrapping around, clutching

holding each other close
*elephants never forget, elephants are
loyal and devoted* the way family
should be, never   divided

the tree we climbed on became
a ship, a portal to another world

my father always told me, after I ran
into the cactus once, I never did again

I wove between the cacti soldiers

effortlessly moving between them
like a thread holding us all together

part of my heart will always be
buried   in Albuquerque.

52-B

     my tiny sanctuary
a quiet space on the
corner of Raspberry with
     Japanese cherry trees
blossoming to welcome early spring
        a breathtakingly bright pink
rainbow crystals echo & spark
     through the rooms, an angelic
        whisper of serenity, safety.

wayfinding / wayfaring

how do you find yourself
    where do you go?
it's all about the journey
I suppose —but what happens
when we no longer know
the path to follow; what happens
to our feet? do we lead in the
same dance, or do we carve out
a new pathway, a new way
of walking through the forest
and the woods.

my body is saying

    be kind to me.
practice compassion in every move (*s l o w*)

be gentle to me; respect me &
hold me with complete love

the universe is saying: be aware
practice mindful manifestation
in every thought & breath

there is not always a reason
but there is always a lesson

my body says *listen*, and I will
tell you all our secrets

I will hold you when everything else
soars aways like a fierce waterfall

I will be here always to cradle your
Soul; to guide you home

my body is saying *welcome*, I am
glad you are here. Stay awhile,

we will discuss Hope and how to
Believe in our abilities.

new skin

    stepping into that new skin I thought
might scar —felt like I could touch the whole
world swirled in the arch of my foot, that tender
sunrise-pink of regeneration. there is growth &
birth all around me— this morning I watched
as an eastern kingbird fetched bits of cut grass
dried then soaked through with rainwater.
we are boundless— everywhere we see
a creation of a new Universe; where we are
master, creator, goddess. claiming these new skins
as if we aren't imposters with stolen identities
already gazing at a foreign reflection, wondering
which character we should portray today?
    is there an end to the seeking?
      the praying? the yearning?
        Or do we just
          let it all
            burn

Selkie

when the sage flowers blossom purple
tipped in royal crowns dripping gold
    late spring, marked by shadows

upon the garden walls at dusk . . .
I want to grab my skin and run,
down to the waves, the edge of the world

where the waters are eager to devour my feet
and welcome me home. a universe awaits,
coral-studded caverns, sea-embellished cities

if only I could return.

    slipping easily into my silky-smooth sealskin
    floating away on the ocean tides, forgotten
    to these frozen heart-lands forevermore.

opossum magic

I ran into an opossum on the path
a soul symbol of resilience, nurturing
the inner child, and walking
alongside your shadow.

abundance, beauty, and a sprinkling
of chaos for good measure—this is how
I   sparked back to life.

for all the times I have grown lost, I've
always found mySelf again. stronger,
brighter, bolder; more authentic
than before.

we are all tiny microcosmic
universes, wrapped in flesh &
bones, blood & brain.

seemingly insignificant
yet echoing complexities
in infinite patterns.

decomposition of a tree

(*in everything, I see you.*)

and the decomposition of a tree
reveals the beauty in death; entire
ecosystem built around the life cycle
ending (*anew. beginning.*) fungi unfold
minty-lace and emerald moss. rhythmic
peck, peck peckpeckpeckpeck~peckpeckpeck
as sapsuckers leech the sweet juices
from tree veins and woodpeckers
tuck food beneath bark before
winter. barred owls nest in hollowed
trunks and raise young with large yellow
eyes and a curious glance. everywhere,
insects are writing spirals like ancient
hieroglyphics on the inside of the tree.
         a snag stands with
branches bare and bold; for long after a tree
begins to die, it enters a new century—just as those
we love and lose remain with us, alive in the
glorious sunsets and infinite, twinkling laughter

of stars.

~ for MomMom

infinity lotus

with brave modesty on my lips,
the winter-sweet kiss of vermouth
and flytrap *nepenthes* —"no sorrow"
I am embittered, acerbic and biting.

crawl inside my magenta-spotted throat
caught in my honeyed web, thick as silk
where was once my tongue. divine
nourishment—salvation.

manifestation

on these crisp, early fall mornings
when I wake up alone, naked

wrapped in sheets like mummified limbs
or a fly caught in the spider's web;

maybe, indeed, even the spider herself
waiting at the center of her intricately

woven lace home... if I am silent,
patient, I may catch the perfect prey.

tears shimmer like raindrops hung
upon the silken strands, vibrating with

an inner hum, a chant...

4:00 am - December

I wonder if my neighbors hear
the howling sobs of a grown woman
through the thin walls of my apartment

oh, it aches at 4:00 am

I don't know how to reckon it all
within me, so here I am //
aching in front of you,
blistered by a midnight sun

counting the days,

the months until my freedom,
ticking time off in my mind
like a metronome.

hibernation

my body grows weary, steps lagged
as the winds begin to howl and blow
the trees bend and sway their wintery waltz.

when the wind creates a second snow

the scent of old-growth forest in early evening,
moss and soil—fireflies as bright luminaries
lit golden along the silent path, bursting

from a sea of flames, tails
blazing like meteorites in flight.

icicles on my   [edges]

we stomped back inside, our feet
covered in snow, and left our boots
kicked off at the door —ice-melt.
your smile warmed me just as much
as your lips —with each frostbitten
kiss, the simple joys of hand-packed
snowballs biting against rosy cheeks
eyes lit with inner fires of love-mischief
a quiet, steady desire —the way
the snowdrift happens almost
before you know it. we may have
barred up our windows and doors
but it's never enough to barricade
love from seeping through the cracks
icicles forming around the edges
of your heart until you don't recognize
the sound of birds who serenade
every morning as the sun splits
the horizon. when all you want
is to be swept off your feet
and all the world offers you is ice,
melt into me —become my new skin,
there's always a place you can
try to squeeze to fit, always a place
you can call home.

the foxes

cross my path
like a compass needle
tails straight, eyes ahead—
unconcerned with my presence

like a compass needle
I am of no relevance
unconcerned with my presence
or importance to the fox family

I am of no relevance
their fur flickering through
or importance to the fox family
the forest like sparks of fire.

their fur flickering through
tails straight, eyes ahead—
the forest like sparks of fire
cross my path.

after-notes

I am uncontainable
and i will shrivel away here
in the shadows, only wanting
a shred of light.

why must I always beg for scraps
of your love, small tokens broken
between teeth like fake silver.

is there any part of my heart
that you consider crystalline?
any part you didn't want to leave
    scarred?

the moth // the flame

do not be the moth
flocking toward destruction.
be the flame withstanding pain
     burning bright
to fend off the darkness
with your sheer light.

do not be the moth
singeing your wings
so you may no longer fly.
be the flame, impenetrable.
feed off the oxygen which
makes you want to stay alive.

do not be the moth
returning to your agony.
be the flame, dancing,
your body flickering
     in the wind.
be the flame, igniting and

consuming all obstacles
in your path.

Dear Winter,

as the first glimpse of frost
gently hangs on tree limbs
I welcome you into my bones
where you can curl up and warm
yourself beside this inner fire

with each puff of breath
that fogs the air, a promise
of all that's to come
generated from the earth as it
slumbers, so much life beneath
snow-covered grounds.
      so much hope.

the belly of winter cradles me
so I can rejuvenate, hibernate
and burst full of blossoming growth
when spring flows in on a breeze
I catch a whiff on the air
and know that winter has left
an everlasting grip to be seen
in the ephemerals and meadows.

II

WORM MOON

the whispers of wolves

it begins as a whisper
    a whisper of wolves
winding among strong trunks of trees
their roots interconnected webs,
intricate & delicate as a spider's
woven deep beneath the earth
if you lay your ear down, listen
to the heartbeat-rhythm of this planet
you'll begin to recognize the pattern
of your own heart, your own yearnings
inexplicably woven between the trees,
the roots and stems, bark and berries,
the boughs that quake and break
and those that hang sturdy high
above our heads or even deep
beneath our underwater grave
dark as a cavern. I venture further
until the light above me no longer exists
discover it within me, radiating outward
touching all in reach—purple afterglow

afterglow

my body is poetry
inviting you to dive in
admire my curves like
metaphors, parentheses of
my hip dips; the commas
of our bodies, our breath
bookending this love—
as fierce as the inner
tides and waves, sonar sounds
of lovemaking— a crescendo,
an earthquake, a waterfall
of cascading emotions.
the way I cried before you
scattered my fears.
                        you offer me
                          sanctuary
for a weary soul, peace
and love without condition.
the purple glow of the sunset
amid the clouds, a nautical
twilight enticing us home
to each other's shelter.

Inchoate Dreams: Rooted

now that I have grown my roots
I am able to stand tall as a tree,
flourish out into the canopy -

to take up the space I am owed
the space I've sought to expand.
rivers of rippling rhizomes sink deep

into the muddy earth, deeper toward
the fiery core. *where does my past
end and the present begin?* in

this intersection of transitions
the future looms ahead, and I—
now tall and wise as a sycamore—

stand sturdy in my grounding, feel
into my source. knowing with certainty
this is the path I am meant to find.

this is my home I am creating.
this is my destiny I am embracing.
this is me. a being of the forest,

the tendrils and branches that grasp
the hawk soaring overhead, calling

from treetops. the mushrooms blooming

from darkened soils—this softly falling
darkness which illuminates all that exists,
all that flowers, sprouts, and seeds

germinating in rich layers, their wrinkles
a time-map tracing where they've tried
to root, in soil without water—in parched

desert lands before we find the lush
undergrowth, ferns fondling ankles
as we wander among this fairy world

walking beside our heart's natural
habitat, meadows of melodic creatures
frolicking through the grass.

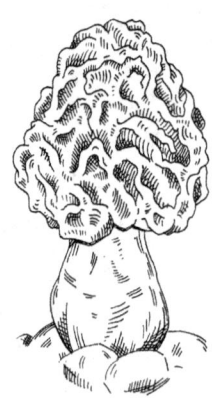

I'll follow

the way we move is like
a calm stream, delicate motion
controlled as a mirror reflection
(*I'll follow you, Body, wherever you go*).
the air flowing through my lungs
a warm breath, a cloud of love
billows out to surround us like a
blizzard, gentle and glorious
sweeping us out to sea in a ship
of joy, floating warm and golden
as we greet the horizon, a rainbow
arching high overhead.

elderberry

there is something wild within me
that I will never tame, a call to
dance free of any chains.
a liberation in limbus...
a howl into the dead of night
without expecting an answer,
a voracious roar and devotion
to passion. to seeking that which
makes us feel alive.

melliferous

*(adj., producing
or yielding honey)*

waking up with last night's lipstick
staining my lips like claret
a darker desire awakens within
as I stretch each limb, test this
human skin before I rampage
through the woods again...

Ravening

        the needs of the wolf beckon
        like a beacon from the forest

moon-sighs and thick thighs
wrap the trunk of you, your roots
deep inside me become a promise
~ to be claimed ~ but if you think
you'll ever extinguish the wild spark
within—think again.

my new gravity

I've had to convince myself of love
countless times before, but you...
you bring me a soft kind of love,
a quiet quickening of the heart,
your scent lingering on my pillows
and the way my lips mold to yours
sweet and true... blue electricity
like live wires jolts between us
you shocked me back to life
a new orbit, my new center of

    gravity.

autumnal abundance

monarchs migrating over
half-mown meadows
a bright flash of gold—
    the final leaf
hanging on limbs of a tree...
this is me, floating. listless
and liminal.
    inflated with light;
as full as the moon radiant
behind clouds, a shimmer.

ready to fall despite the drop,

    ready
    to let you catch me
    on the way
    down.

tremolo

the eye of the forest
is always watching
the leaves of her trees
always wound within your hair
her bark grown like skin

radiant tones through the
trees like a tremolo

the call of the spirit
echoes eternal

[dating...] for wolf women

common human in silken moonlit
skin stretched tight over bones

missing warm fur as I slide inside a fitted dress,
lace & velvet falls delicate over broad shoulders.

there are benefits to being human, I think
as I twirl & admire myself in the mirror

I might consider myself beautiful
if not for the danger I see when I look deep inside

my glinting golden wolf-eyes: *untamed.*

ephemeral

like an ephemeral, she blooms
in the early spring morning-dew
her petals unfurl quietly, slowly
reaching out to feel the touch of the
sun, its graceful yet fervent heat.

how does she release a love
once ingrained so deep
on every bone, in every nerve...
circulating like soul-essence, like a
nefarious poison leeching away;
it blackens the heart
and rots the core
there's no visible mark
yet the words left
scars upon her heart

how does she learn to love
again...? to trust?
just as spring ephemerals
bloom each season despite
knowing their time will be
fleeting; the embrace of the
sun, the wind and the nourishing
rains are enough. to enjoy,
even for a little while.

glimmers

catch the wolf's reflection
in the gold-trimmed full length
mirror and smile, twirl. do a little
dance in this earthly form, ethereal.
a room of thistles and trumpet flower
holds tight to your soul, cradles you
for the moment, rocks you with a
lullaby of bare skin, ruffled fur,
golden eyes and a silver tongue
sharp as a knife.

> *there's a shimmer in her eyes*
> *as she spreads those thic thighs*
> *exalting in the beauty of a silhouette*
> *this flesh & bone that cages soul*
> *a proclamation, to all that makes us*
> *whole/Full.*

l i m b o

these languid months between the winter
    like hungry mouths of baby birds
begging for a worm, regurgitated from the
    belly of the Universe, a galaxy
existing lightyears beyond any comprehension
    there's a blackhole somewhere
waiting to eat us all alive in a flash of light
    no more than a burst, a speck of
extraordinary embers going out in one final
    gasp... in my dreams, I'm always
running away from the predicted fate   (demise)
    even when I have no idea who is
chasing at my heels—maybe this blackhole
    itself, kicking stardust in its wake.

cosmos

in this endless chase, the hunt continues
even as the day breaks over crusted eyelids.
we welcomed the new year in by the throat,
claimed this decade as our own as we howled
in each other's tongues, this love language
only we speak now, our secret lovemaking
to celebrate the birth of a new cosmos
within ourselves.

nautilus

I want to be like the ammonite
spiraling onward, collecting new
growth with each year, learning to
live with my past but not dwell in it.
I want to be like the wind
ever-blowing and resilient yet
still calm and present even in
the sight of leaves in the tree canopy,
I want to be like the rocks
so steady in who they are, yet
willing to soften to the acts of
nature and the courses we are
on, these cyclical seasons and
the way a rock lodged in the
riverbed will begin to take on that
form, the rivulets embody and
embrace this movement and
still, they endure. I want to be
like the ephemerals in spring
blossoming up from the earth to
greet the sun after frost has
vanished from the land —before
returning to rest and nourish
the earth they grow and rely on.
I want to be like the birds
unafraid to sing their song or

find their voice —that early
morning reminder that life is
a beautiful bounty waiting to
behold. I want to be like the oak
trees, the sycamore and birch that
rise tall above the rest, unashamed
of all they may carry and the
witnessed pasts they hold; strong
and sure of all they want most to
become. I want to be like the
growing fern, first a tiny enclosed spiral
before unfurling and growing to
my full height, absorbing the power
of the sunshine and grace of starlight.
I want to be like the moon, weightless
in the night sky's orbit and whole
no matter what light shines down,
I am radiant beyond belief —
learning to live again, learning to
breathe again. opening my heart,
mind, body, soul —back up to love,
grace, passion —and joy. the
beautiful way nature knows to
show up, to promise dedication
and courage to continuous growth.
boundless ventures. infinite journeys.

silent forest meditations

purple flowers, bits off tree.
a deep red color called to me;

I picked up a dogwood petal
and carried it along the path,

      then another
      which I released
      to the creek
      along with the
      burdens of my past.

ammonite heart

heart like a spiral, a pinecone,
the ammonite fossil —allowing growth
and malleability.   I wish my heart to
always expand, regenerate, and grow,
to remain endlessly open, arcane
and layered.   I wish my heart
to know   there is so much room
for its authentic growth,   this layered
healing —we do not ever stop loving
or desiring to be-loved.

never abandon the wild within you;
it is cherished and desired.

war paint

        decorate my body   in war paint

crimson to show   i've walked through
                    the fires of hell & still
                          come out alive *

indigo because   i am not afraid of drowning
                  and still possess / the hottest
                    part of the flame where I left
                  myself
                        burning / incendiary. *

emerald to represent   i have laid down
                        like the grass,
                        been walked upon
                              but still risen. *

rose-gold since   my skin is gilded
                  even if it does not glow,
                        it is still precious. *

coal black as if   i have been consumed by
                  the darkness that clutches
                  & possesses me despite the light
                    of day / still luminescent. *

* you cannot claim me or break me.
[*only I can do that to myself.*]

to you, i will never
surrender

dreams of mud & fire

the days have been soaked in rain,
cloud cover, dreams of mud & fire
    waking me in spurts.
       not every day
is easy —some hurt worse. I try not
  to radiate my own pain outward.
each day is heavier healing, spitting
    out of me like lava.

Laniakea

in a spark of iridescent rage
      radiating from the base of my neck
(*reptilian*) —I flung the slice of moonbeam
across the sky, cracking into spiderwebs of
crystallized lightning inviting us to peer inside
other realms, other timelines, other galaxies
a constantly expanding universe unfolds
spiraling out from a seed of spiteful vengeance.

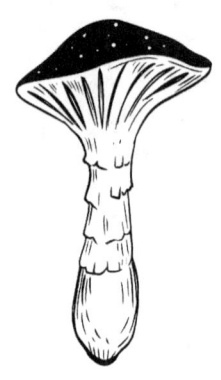

stretch marks

my favorite thing about my body
this year are my sTrEtCh mArKs
the way they decorate my thighs
lightning bolts like heaven
come down to lick my skin
leaving an imprint of love and
healing: a trail-map to follow
as you blindly dive into the forest
hoping only to come out alive.

Like a River

> *how do you fall in love?*
> *harder than a bullet could hit you*
> *how do we fall apart?*
> *faster than a hairpin trigger*
>
> *~ Bishop Briggs*

this transition feels quiet,
centered at the heart of me
yet, tumultuous as a raging river.
I know a bit better where I'm
traveling. I know a bit more of
who I am. & most importantly
this year, I know how to seek
the love I so desire and crave,
to claim it for my own... both
that soft, internal love and
the hardened, eternal love
of finding someone who
loves me unconditionally.

mulberry

and when there is so much pain
I can barely breathe, I ask the earth
beneath me, steady partner; the air
around me, constant friend; and the
trees that stand tall, constant
support... to take this pain and ease it
out from my womb like a thread, bury it
like a needle. out from the basin of my
spine... out from the keyholes of my hips.

III

FLOWER MOON

luna moth

moon-drenched rituals lit by
sage smoke; strawberry full.
replenish this tired body, soak
my soul in the gaze of night—

this nakedness begging for a
touch of magic, the goddesses'
light lent once I ground into
these earthen powers; flight.

(woman) of the woods

I am of the trees, *crescere*—
bark skin ripples in reed-thin winds
belly echoes with the sun's eternal ache
a seed planted—*rót, radix* (rooted)
// I am infinitely reaching....
    above
      &
    below.

soul-patching in paradise

> *for Gould Lake.*

full moon basking over dark waters
loon calls across the lake, silent
trees and a rocky mountain
      juts over the waters rippling in
      moonlight.

all is peace, calm—
      tranquil.

in the morning,
a broad-winged hawk calls from
the distant treetops, a crow and
black squirrels dart among the
trees and roots. a loon basks
in the middle of ripples, bobbing
for fish   trills.
hummingbird wings   coyotes
yipping near the distant mica mines.
barred owls singing lullabies
through the trees.

traverse

trying to define who we are
is a vast and never-ending challenge
but we pick up pieces along the way,
we meet people who we want to stay,
and we learn to love who we are
even when we fear nobody else will

we learn the value in honoring our authenticity
we learn how to stand up for what we believe
and what we crave, the ways we need
to be loved, cherished, and honored.

just like seeing the sunset and its afterglow
of deep purple, magenta, and orange
transports me to another time, another place
where all I am is breath, all I am is body.

all I am is earth & as I become back to the heart
of me, back to the bone, I am the rushing water
beside the trail, the rock rising high above.

I am the crash of salt and sand,
I am the rebirth. I am the nautilus, the spiral.

full moon romp

wolf needs.

yes, we have darkness
& must wield it with
care, for it can destroy
and create much chaos.

his fingers draped around
the steady pulse
thundering at my throat.

learning the language of birds

we begin the morning with gentle bird walks among large oaks and fledgling trees, juniper... a monarch butterfly perches beside the creek; another on a burst of delicate purple weed. the morning tastes tangerine, saccharine as we tread along; a kingfisher arches overhead, two goldfinches twirl together in a tree. a silent indigo bunting flashes by, as startling in its beauty as the female Baltimore oriole who flashes overhead orange-yellow like quick lightning. later, as we check an open nest box and score the sides to help fledgling sparrows escape, we glimpse the orchard oriole who had been calling to us across the meadow—his wings glint like copper in the sun as his entire body thrusts with the passion of his song. the language of birds is one I learn slowly, first spending time training my ears before I can imagine speaking with them, walking in reverence among their territory, basking in the light and lilted grace of their songs.

— for D.B., thank you
for the lessons

esculent

fit to be eaten.

a few mornings after I planted
our veggie garden, I went out
to see a spider weaving her web
intricately, one strand at a time
endlessly looping back around
to create this home. so subtle &
elusive, not even my camera
could capture that delicate web-
weaving; a moment all our own

the spider, & me.

impetus

plant yourself deep into
the root of me,
I embrace your stem
      and flourish out
like monstera leaves

heady elevation

there's a crack like molten lava
breaking through my chest cavity...
a cavernous vacancy where [   ]
used to be. I already let [   ] go
by the time [   ] wanted me back
    all I could say was no...

what was broken between [   ]
lies cracked, gleaming, and magnetic
as that lava flow beckoning [   ] closer
just a touch.   a single taste on the
    tip of my tongue or finger,

the way i've been burnt before
by this lustful adoration...

sequoia promises // gingko season

you walk beside me
   & I'll walk beside you.
from the first moment we locked eyes
I knew you were special.

[[*my heart is giant as a sequoia*
 sturdy in the ever-present breeze
 layered as the colors of a gingko
 before it sheds all its leaves...]]

the way your presence ignites me
is a sure sign we were meant
to meet, beyond time and space
that fateful day I walked into your

life and you swept me off my feet,
when I knew I'd manifested you
—the way you kissed me
let me know you are the one.

meditations of a budding plant mom

my green thumbs drip gold
coating stems with syrup-sap
of new growth; each new leaf
that bursts forth to embrace
tendrils of light—regenerating
like language on the tongue
forgotten long enough to turn sour
/ prickly pear poison or soft as
a velvety philodendron leaf \
even my plants speak only poetry
there is a whispered love between us
as my fingertips trace patterns
learning how to read their veins
and a finger stuck down in their soils
helps to monitor their root-growth,
like pale ghosts alive under dirt, an
intricate network of life like upside-
down breathing, or a heart beating
beneath the earth. my desires
are full of fiery anger. stoked with
loss, another heartache before i
open, vulnerable and glistening,
reaching for the sun on my face,
seeking kisses on my upturned lips
just as my growing jungle thrives
beneath a patient, gentle touch.

summer azure

butterfly speckled white wings
but when they flash open wide
they spark silver to my eye,
forest enchantress, leading you
astray beside the runoff in a
blossoming avalanche of rhododendrons
pushing forth their deep emerald leaves
their bright pink-and-white hopeful blooms.

murmuration

there's a meditation in hanging
freshly washed bedsheets on the line
in the earlyspring air, still crisp
with a taste of winterbite
then watching their pale dance
floral and etched in the wind
wavering, never faltering to pick
up and meet the wind in its waltz
each fancy footstep... and languished
sigh.

moonspeak

I lay beneath the dark-clouded cobalt skies
communing with the trees while we caught
whispers of the wind; really—*whispers of wolves*
through the tall bluestem grasses. they whisper
as gentle as wildflowers poking up
through the meadow.

can you hear the moonspeak
ginger-tipped shadows & cinnamon

interlude

a wolf woman bites back
her howl—so as not to wake
the pack... this moment is only
hers, a sacred recognition
of all that remains
to be claimed, caressed—

a chest-deep beckon,
full-throated wail.

palimpsest

to rewrite the past with our future
ingrained like old scars on weathered paths
a stormcloud ready to break, burst—unable to
hold the rain within it. a new lover
paving new avenues of pleasure between
lustful thighs/sighs. can you ever rewrite
the scars or will they always exist like
the scorned love of two divorced lives
two divorced hearts, yet always—
the memory of love lingers.

heartwood

    the cacophony of crows in the
        early morning
the mournful cry of loons across
a quiet midnight lake
waves lap against shore here as a
        lullaby or a promise
of all your desires fulfilled, worries washed
clean away... like a thunderstorm
rolling in over the lake's calm surface
baring your nude body to the lake and
sunshine, the early morning birdsong
as you stretch and dance, exalt in
your human form and the wild wolf
captivating you. beckon in the storm,
ask it to sweep you up in loving embrace
a chariot of thunder, a stampede of rain horses
empress charting across the sky like a meteor

the night I became a nudist

the blood-orange moon rose
in the sky like a drop of
pomegranate juice as we drove
away from our liberation,
cresting dark hillsides and chasing
that brilliant moon... a bright
fireball meteor streaked across the
black, where we lay naked in a field
and blinked at the stars, breathing
in and out, all these promises
of joy, peace, togetherness, body
love...   I took his
body in my hands, & all felt right
two puzzle pieces (re)joining
as he pushed deep inside me
and we rode against the
climaxing tides, a blanket of
stars heady above us, tiny dots
as millions of lights, a holy
devotion to living life to its fullest
suckling every last drop
from the nectar of existence.

dragon-toothed

if i could show up as anything...

I would show up bold and unashamed,
uninhibited by anyone's expectations and
so much larger than my own ingrained beliefs.
I would show up as a dragon, my scales
sparkling and mysterious. I would
show up with flames roaring between
parted lips, jagged teeth and a promise
of acceptance alongside this transitional
journey. I would be raging and beautiful,
unstoppable in my fearlessness. I would
honor every emotion evoked within
my body, offering it space to explore,
expand and exalt. even the most fleeting
emotions deserve time to live and experience
the rush of life. I would discover comfort
in my own rhythms, the quiet mediation
of fixing a cup of tea or lingering with a
book, the light playing between leaves in the
tree limbs above, the wind a sacred whisper,
the leaves falling to the ground, the speckled
shimmer as nature catches us each time we're
ready to fall, to foster new growth as the seasons
change; life offers a change to spread those
infinite wings and soar past any limitations.

my Perseids man

came to me like a sparking comet
entering my atmosphere, ablaze
with light, a great ball of fiery embers
igniting me back to life. I'd gone dim,
my light near-extinguished, flickering
until your spark lit me bright.

> the way embers continue
> to burn long after the flame
> is extinguished. this is the
> way I love you—enduring,
> persistent and warm on the
> rainiest evenings; my love
> shoots like meteors through
>
> > a moonlit sky, a night
> > categorized by stars.

dark & stormy: *a symphony*

with parted lips, her declarant
howl an evocative cry through the night;
blue lace agate at her collarbone.

    while the beast lies dormant in his den
    sated after fulfilling his dark feast,
    the wolf remains wakeful, watchful.

        undettered from keeping ears perked
        & golden eyes wide as a full moon,
        illuminating all that dares cross

            her threshold, or that of
            anyone
                she loves.

the muse

...something called me back...
             { where is my mind }
to the time before when
we danced hand in hand
beneath the trees and he
promised me always...

but also, to that first time
I dared to dance alone
without fear of being seen
and my feet found the steps
as if they'd known them all
along. my body knew the way

before my mind could second-
guess it, ruin the rawness—
the reality of that ripple within
like the one I saw that day
stretched on a canvas amidst
an artist's handmade studio,

all the colors, all the layers
and the light that we refract
with our very eyes. all that
the water, the snow reflects—
each color and movement,

an undertow of opportunity

for the muse to find her pathway
just as she moves, so very
effortlessly, within me.

a new way of living

the water is our calm mirror,
the stars my nautical blanket
as birds echo overhead.

I am full of life, radiance—
sun-kissed, wind-swept, sandy
and salt-dressed. wild & free.

a wolf on the bayside, howling
her serenade.   I am weightless,
a buoy.

      elegant, moving out from
caliginous forests, I discover
new ways of living, breathing;

devouring each moment
to mold into a memory—
tasting it like a pearl

formed tenderly
on my tongue.

after the storm

I am the rainbow after
    the wildest storm
I am the eye of the rain drop,
    the universe within
I am ready to embrace all
    that awaits for me.
my present may be uncertain
    but I am leaning into the unknown
shedding all energies not meant
    for this new birth
in preparation for an intense
    metamorphosis
I welcome all my higher self
    has been waiting for me to recognize.
burst free. bloom. become.
    finding myself over and over,
rebirthing who I will be.

IV

BUCK MOON

the caterpillar

dances as it creates its chrysalis,
  many days it waits, works
before becoming the butterfly
  when it can spread its wings
to all it has been storing,
  manifesting, and creating.

(vernal) marshlands

in the marshlands
    where the wild has crept in &
        found solace in the clutch of
            knowing *there is a place for each & every*
                creature... lily pads create
a bridge
    for frogs & other amphibious beings
        an ethereal crossway for dragonflies
            & Fairies   to enter our ephemeral
                realm...

wild terrains

life is one huge manifestation, our beings a creative
process. I'm in the act of shedding—*so many layers*—
all who I thought I'd become; & who I became, to survive.

who I used to think I'd be; who I needed to be to pull
myself out on the other side... (none of it is who I
thought I'd be). I am

                softer than expected. quieter,
more content with isolation; less called to technology.
less called even to safe spaces once used for healing;

I am carving out new homes, new safe dwellings
unconditional love hollows me out, heals wounds
I barely catalogued

                now, it's about recognizing
how worthy I am, of this love. of this life.
this new sanctuary I am threading with bare hands

and a trembling heart. *you are so worthy*, I tell myself;
no matter what false narratives you hold. release
your need for perfection; to be fully healed, or 'whole'.

this is the whole. our unhealed selves, our parts
that cry out for attention, for adoration. we are

all of this, and more. this is the journey.

    the JOURNEY.

so often, we have our destination in mind, a fabrication of who we will be when we are "healed," or "whole" when in reality we are walking ourselves to an unknown

goal, each step has meaning, purpose. each step brought us here, now. relish those steps—feel their weight. their heat.

    there is so much   yet to discover,
        so much   yet to mend.

I am learning what home feels like.

what having a place of my own
feels like. living by my own time,
my own desires. I am carving out

a sanctuary to rest, rejuvenate my
soul, and discover what it really means
to feel safe, and on my own. to cultivate

friendships (and good friends who bring
housewarming jade plants, for longevity)
and to relearn myself, who I am and

who I'm becoming, who I will be.
don't we all do this dance through life
where we fumble, we stumble—we fall

into love sometimes with the wrong people
on our way to hopefully finding the right
we lose our footing but yet we gain it again

on higher ground, conquering mountains.

celebrating the big and small wins;
the success, support, and solo living
a pathway home, to self-discovery.

giants of the forest

*there is a great & wild
awakening within me*

*rumbling, tumbling
through the wilderness*

the seductive smile that freedom
of spirit brings (begging you
to take my hand as I lead you

astray in the forest of deep desire,
lustful lichen...) will you follow
me? trust again (or for the first

time) the offered heart of another
~ fear & desire often feel familiar,
if not the same ~ so how do i

know you'd meet my howl
with all i want most deeply
unless i first meet it within myself,

discover the power i need
to dance alone to the beat
of your heart-drums // remedy

the rhythm beating ragged inside
my heartline... the cymbals chime,
entice me to shed defenses ((*but*

*what is it that makes me feel
safe...?*)) riddle me this new
symphony i've started to sing;

you fit into every new melody.

the rest is yet to be discovered
music still to be composed
though i know the notes I'd

like you to play—your name
on the tip of my tonuge; and
mine, caught in the back of

your throat, tapped out in every
      thump of your heart.

ghost fern

on the saccharine days of summer
the hint of spring still in the air
all that new growth, all that rebirth

kicked up from the soil's depths
like Persephone kicking her heels
in a joyous dance of freedom from

the underworld... all the ways we
learn to weather the tides, and then how we
g e n t l y learn how to breathe again;

a collection of glimmers like rainbows
sweet & savory as they melt on my tongue.

desert thunderstorm

I'm quivering in anticipation
of the day your fingers undress me –
    delicate or a ripping,
tearing to get to flesh / pulp beneath.

use your teeth / scrape against
engraved lines of my body / trace
each dipping curve with fingertips.

this is the way I want
you to become my lover –
gentle at first / but then
with fervent passion.

open my eyes / with a gasp
to worlds I've never seen,
endless nights / making love beneath
stars / limbs entwined

my blood effervescent / like
sweet champagne bubbling.

how will it feel – this taking / joining of
ardent flesh & tongues & breath?

thunderstorm devouring in great

crescendo / like the desert loves
the sand consuming it
your hands memorize
each crevice / your eyes
drink me in

at the end / when we must part
take a piece of me / an offering
to be kept,
> *always.*

I am one with my pack & my pack is one with me

trekking through the swamps of Pinchot Trail,
I chant this mantra to myself while perching on mossy logs
fallen and reclaimed by lichen, mushrooms of all kinds
sprouting from their bark. it's hushed in this peatmoss
boggy marshland, rhododendron bushes lining our path.
our breath fogs the air on our first real morning, (the
weather predicted snow), and we feel tiny dots of sleet
begin to hit our faces as we climb the mountainous terrain.
I am one with my pack & my pack is one with me—
it's the third time I say it that my partner turns and says,
smiling, "that refers to wolves, too." we've come to an
emerald grove of old oaks and pines. the moss grows here
the color of electric limes as sunlight filters through
the canopy. breath-taken, we follow along the creek
in a rare silent moment, our feet easily finding the trail,
often padded by moss, our packs swaying gentle
on our backs. if we listen close, the trees also sway and creak
in the powerful winds, our bodies only slightly sheltered
from its howls. eventually we will come to a rushing
waterfall, roaring down the banks, carrying into the stream
and we will sit by it, our backs arched into the rocks
as we smoke a joint, admire the pure beauty of nature.
I am one with my pack, and my pack is one with me.
as I swing on rhododendron-bush limbs and narrowly
avoid the muck, I begin to feel one with nature, too,
and how we return to who we really are the more we
integrate ((like tree roots)) back to our genuine soils.

unFURling like a fiddlehead

first clutched tight to the ground
(spiralhead tucked down)
gentle breath of spring chases away
frost-barren lands; the gentle golden
glow like sunshine bursting from
      its shroud

I have grown a strong pelt
layered with memories, a gardenbed
of *déjà vu* where I've projected
my soul to this place of safety,
wholeness. at times, I am even
content.

anamnesis

where the philodendron dark lord
witnesses every last stretch of sunlight
glimmering between the trees, and

my heart trills along to the
cicadian rhythm as they chirp
and sing a song of sex & early

death—this is their destiny.
a flood of fireflies dances
across the grass. though i

know i've seen these things
many times before, each
moment brings a certain

type of breathless, childlike
wonder.

wolf fangs

hair whipping violet in the wind
she shifts in secret by the light
of each sunrise/set—back to human
flesh & bone, before daylight
touches dew-frosted tips.

signs of self-reliance

a bald eagle swooped down holy,
breaking water with two curled talons
as it gripped a fish and leapt into the air
a peregrine falcon called, cresting its zenith

since reborn into the wild, a brood found
along the falls, white speckled chest; black-
tipped feathers & piercing huntress eyes.
an osprey nest perched atop a metal bridge

& the locks—great big canal barges with oysters
spitting lake water as I latch onto each ladder rung,
a claw gripping all 8,000 tons to the edge of the wall
      like grasping to the edge of the galaxy.

the storm rolled in black-purple velvet that night
rocked us gently in our mooring and lit the night
sky amethyst, edged purple like a deep/dark
wine swirled in the glass and

gulped down in one swallow,
                      replaced by obsidian.

The Wolf Queen

regrounding, remembering, rebirthing the soul.

there is a pure magic found in the beauty of leaves
falling while you stand among the forest,
the trees tall and whispering.

here, I find myself. my soul.
here, the earth speaks in quiet wind-trills
and the soft ethereal patterns of leaves
as they dance; an infinite waltz and
serenade to the winter that will come.

today, the veil is thin. our manifestations
become reality. our energies align with soul.
be kind, be gentle, be graceful.

dream-quaking

wake from reveries of sludge
& smoke; dream-quakes vibrate
larger than life;   *i am trapped.*

sleep plagued by nightmares
leaves me whimpering, fetal
though I've vanquished

many demons in my lifetime
present anxieties still morph
in monstrous forms to torment

    the deep, dusky night.

breathing underwater

>*you're slowly*
>>*opening back to life.*

a mantra for us all on the days we feel
like a slowly unfurling flower, our petals
uncurling to the sun's embrace… a week

spent on the peaceful shores of Gould Lake,
a Canadian wilderness meditation, a solace
and embrace of solitude and awareness—

our natural rhythms and the spirals we climb,
ascend to the top even as we know we might
crumple to the ground again. even as we know

love might rip our hearts out, leave them beating/
leave them bleeding. even as we know life
may not always offer us what we most hope for.

all we can do is carry on, embracing each emotion
for all its indigo tides, its pull as heavy as the moon
intense as this magnetic, gravitational love…

the way of water

the way of water is to
show you all the fluid ways
one can exist. the ebb, the flow
the ripple and tides—caught
in a circling current spiraling
outward and in. the loon & her
baby sitting atop the lake;
the flight of the blue heron
lifting off from the shore...
the dance like a twirl of your lover
as you swing barefoot on
the grass, the taste of summer
& sweat. the salting tears
rushing down your cheeks,
the words "I love you"
caught in the back of your
throat. the way we move
forward, a rush and a beckon
and as we let go, the adrenaline
of something new to come...

Blue Lake

we paddle out to the lake inlet, all six of us
plus two dogs. one of us 8-months pregnant
with the next generation of our family.

paddling against the current, the wind
we move together smoothly across the lake,
destined for our spot on a hidden side

where we pick up our kayaks, paddleboards,
and one canoe, setting down in the waters
of Blue Lake, a perfect fishing spot.

when I catch the behemoth bass, he swings
my paddleboard in the water, pulling me
so at first I think I've latched to a stick

but when I reel him in, his mouth looks
big enough to gulp me down and I hold on
with all my weight as I call for help.

the moment we return to shore, I'm eager
to fillet him. my brother stands by, helps
guide me as I smoothly slide the knife

beneath layers of skin, skirting the spine
and working among the blood and guts

to pull the meat from bone. ripping the scales

and peeling them back, preparing the fish
which we'll eat that night, prepping in a pan
with garlic and white wine—the flavor of the lake

warm and salty on my tongue; celestial.

the snail

with his spiral-dome shell
clung to the rain-speckled glass
making his way by following light
the pathways of vibration
he curled out from his home
devouring a sliver of grass.
if only life was as simple as:
here, I am travelling, and
making my path, stopping
to enjoy a snack, soaking up
rain drops before I make my
slow descent to the ground,
seeking once more:
      the scent-paths to follow
deep into the gardenbeds,
deep into the night.

wolf den ((building a home))

> *"help me, heal me, tell me*
> *I'm cured;*
> *it's all behind me,*
> *yeah..."*
>
> — LP

two pairs of hands set to build
this foundation (of love), this structure
(of life).   *'cause I feel safe here.*
the only way to build this safety net
is weaving each strand with bare fingers
until they blister, bleed. but still, we build
this home with hands in the dirt, fingernails
stained black after a day in the gardenbed
planting native wildflowers. we sit in the back
garden with a crackling fire in the pit, sticks
and stones lit aflame so they can no longer
break us. (they lied at that part—the words
always hurt the worst). our pain-speak swirls
in the curling spirals of flame, sparks —offering
a steady heat as the spring night cools. our rage
long forgotten, bitten off the tongue like spice.
I want so badly to keep creating this home, my
sanctuary. I want to believe I can heal enough
to embrace every moment as our own.

effulgence

viewing the female bobolink
with her soft golden breast, a slice

of lightning broke the sky's grey
clouds—caught in my binoculars

like a central force. the male bobolink's
black body and flaming yellow head

displays and courts his mate, trilling
a unique song as he flutters and

swoops down low over rainy
grassland meadows. a kestrel

perches on a distant nest; swallows
dance between tall grasses. all is so alive,

a glorious & vibrant ignition.

a study in imperfection

in last night's pottery class
our teacher taught us about clay—
the decomposition of flora & fauna,
naturally forming for 900 million years.
I could smell its earthy essence as I worked
the clay between my fingers, cupping with
my palms, guiding with my thumbs, sculpting
a dance of gravity, movement, and balance.
when the teacher saw my pieces, he smiled
with a wise sparkle in his eye—*remember*,
he said, *what I spoke of at the beginning;
the Japanese art of wabi-sabi*. this is how
they honor and celebrate impermanence,
imperfection of nature and life. my pieces
flowed like the oceanic waves, whipping
beyond my control. as I worked, I learned
how to grip the clay, how to mold. how
to release the need for control—allow the clay
to become what it wants to be, all it
dreams it can be—imperfect, flawed; complete.

indigo tides

> *"you're the sea,*
> *the sky,   deep*
> *as the color*
>
> *indigo."*
>
> — *Bonnie x Clyde*

when the moon   lights the windows
and the mind   races like daring tides

thunderstorm lullabies   soothe my body
back down   from the throes

of despair.

V

HARVEST MOON

tap root

like a seed, we sprout from this earth;
where we set our roots is where we find
our feet deep in the ground—a dark
phantasmagoria of sound, light, peace, flight...
as we become, discover.　　　I run beneath
　　　the street lamps with a howl caught
　　　in my throat; the new moon means
　　　all is quiet, all is dark. hushed...

　　　　　　I rest, in wait. I grow, patient.
　　　　　　there is a salty taste on the tip
　　　　　　of my teeth; a promise of desire
　　　　　　and all that is to come...

I am blossoming

shedding my seasonal pelt
like a ghost pipe, I shrivel
only to come alive & glow

once I've properly rested
monotropa uniflora—I am
forever-wild; untrammeled.

mycelium branching like
scalewort consuming beech
bark; a beautiful devouring.

myrmecochory

    the seashell curve of her spine like a
    whispering ocean, deep secrets spiral
    as you move through the depths of her
    the curl of her hips like fiddlehead ferns
    grasping up for an embrace of light.

the slow burn

comes upon me like a swell
cascading; like ink-caps gradually
melting into something greater

when Atlas shrugged his shoulders
& took on the weight of the world,
the storms of Jupiter swirled

around his head. a snail whose
shell is a skull; the Cheshire smile
& mantra, 'we're all mad here'

over a thudding heart.

a gorilla howling across the belly,
protecting loved ones from any
who dare cross

a coffin opening at the top of the
rib cage, the universe spilling out
& a hand, infinitely reaching...

a reminder: you are never alone.

reminescences

born surrounded by mountains, where I learned
how to step carefully over rattlesnakes on the dirt path
and weave between cacti. moved to a new land, hills
and forests ruled by wildlife.
undergrowth

my body has become a work of art;
tattooed by ink as well as traumas
a journey & map for another to follow

my ammonite a constant reminder: *"live with the past,
but don't dwell in it."* no matter how quickly or
chaotically life seems to spiral out of control,
there's always something beautiful to experience,
witness, or behold.

my fern reminds me to unfurl; never let anyone
keep me tucked tight & small. to branch out, reach
for those who can nurture me; to care for the
understory in the shadows as much as the canopy
thriving high above.

my wild geranium is a love note to native wildflowers,
pollinators, and all that nature provides us daily.
symbolic of peace, love, joy, fertility & spirtuality.
in Scandinavian myth, they're dedicated to Odin—

god of war & poetry.

they are the beauty, however evanescent, that remains at the end of every battle I've fought; the ephemeral that transitions & changes... even the shell & bones we all, inevitably, leave behind.

entwined (the entanglement)

> *"you are a gushing flame*
> *hailing from an eastern sky...*
>
> *you are the first & last name*
> *whispered through the ether.*
>
> *so willfully   destroying,*
> *unlike any other."*
>
> — *King Woman*

your legs like oaken tree trunks
wrapped tight around mine,
infinitely entwined. the rain
that replenished the reservoir
we never suck each other dry;
instead, recharge & rejuvenate
each time our lips meet, it's shared
breath, our yearning to get lost
in deep skin-time unbearable
       to resist.

(scent)-iments

the dawn skies reminded me
of you; the indigo sky was
so beautiful.

I will love you, always,
   as you are.

may you sleep peacefully
with the scent of me
wrapped in your sheets.

if you were to name a
fungi after me... i would
want one that supports

an entire species, tangling
around a tree's roots to
prevent it from dying

or ever lacking
nourishment.

alluvial fan

learning how ex-lovers are for
poetry, where they shall remain
plangent; chained forevermore
shackled by the iron of these lines
trying to jump the stanzas
but they've been eternally
imprinted here; their mark as
black as the deep marsh silt,
dredged for new growth.

hiking alone (a woman in the woods)

i follow a woman on Instagram who solo-
backpacks around the world, a tumor
consuming her brain while she creates
beautiful art & her poetry ignites my own
passions. i wish i could follow in her
footsteps, camping in breathtaking
locations; the mountaintops & amidst
an abundance of fragrant ferns

even the glory of days without showers
dirty legs & split feet would be a blessing
to escape into the wilderness with only
my soul & what I can carry on my back

I am a woman wandering the woods
also alone (though, they don't know
the wolf wanders, always, with me)—
rippling her fur down my spine in times
when my metal waterbottle weapon
may come in too much handy...

deliquesce

> (verb; 1. - to dissolve or melt away;
> 2. - to become soft or liquid with
> age or maturity—used of some
> fungal structures (as the gills
> of a mushroom))

i am ~
flesh & bone
rock-solid earth
made from river beds
……. . . ….
trace me whole,
i become unbroken
in your hands ~ every time.

the meeting: *a love story*

we met along the Pettaqumscutt River
those gentle riptides pulling our kayaks
together; an invisible thread tethering
my heart to yours from the beginning.

the salt marshes lapped against the banks
tall grasses high along either side, where
herons hid—one even perched atop the
tallest tree along the riverbanks

(that elusive, rare white heron who
evaded us still sometimes haunts
my dreams). you spoke to me about
the interconnected systems of nature

& the body; how we are all one...
no man had ever spoken so poetically
to me before; maybe it was the rhythm
of the water or the feral nature I sensed

even then; like a jolt in my chest, you
ignited a passion in the pit of me
not easily ignored or tampered.
our paths interlocked that day,

as I told my companions I'd met

my future husband & my intuition
deep inside told me, *'yes, it's true'*
everything within thrums in response

to your mind, your body, your soul.

moments I want to remember

how still it was in the old-growth forest
when we first said "I love you" beneath
the red oaks covered in lichen.

gazing deep into your eyes, I've never
felt so at home before. my entire body
so at peace. these are moments

I want to remember, forever. the way
you pause in the woods and hover over
fungi & lichen, taking pictures

to create into art. you don't even realize
you're a masterpiece all your own;
the way I'll memorize your patterns

with every gentle caress of my hands.

i dreamt

of growing our own
chantarelles and oyster
mushrooms; their bright
orange & creamy white
flesh blooming, swarming.

i dreamt of a sumac tree's
bursting-full branch breaking
during a storm; the pleasure
i felt knowing i could then
make sumac lemonade.

the oak & his lichen ~

an eternal symbiosis

a grand oak stands atop the mountain
happily enveloped in his lichen; both
enjoying their outlook
of the world

everyday affirmations

I like the idea that I am safe and secure

I am steady like a rock, rooted like a willow.
I sway with the breeze of emotions. I bend
      but I do not break.

I like the idea that I am comfortable in my
      own skin; that no matter
I am always held in these moments of
      uncertainty....

when the world feels unsteady,
when I no longer know my pathway
home, I am under a *realignment*
of heart, body, mind & soul.

    I know at the end of the day
    I am worthy of more than pain;
    I am worthy of great abundance.

I am loved & cherished.

Acknowledgments & Inspirations

To my eternal muse, Stella Storm, who constantly lifts me higher—11 precious years together and many more to enjoy.

To my family, who has stood by me even in the darkest times—my blood pack. To my friends who endure with me, for being my chosen pack.

To the healers of this world; in particular, those who inspired poems in this collection. Most notably, Naila, of This Hallowed Wilderness—for the infinite healing and inspiration found in your grief workshops.

I love you, all.

Some versions of these poems and prose previously published or appeared in: *Reclamation* anthology; *Capsule Stories: Spring 2020* edition.

~ a special dedication ~

to A.M.L. and Moon Pie;

*for holding hands with me
at (what felt like) the end of the world...
may you both Rest in Peace.*

I hope you'd be proud.

purple-purple-red-black-red

MUSICAL MUSES & ARTWORK

"after the storm" —inspired by: Darpan, Kailash Kokopelli, "Metara (Metamorphosis)." *Golden Dragonrider (Alchemy of Mystic Songs and Lullabies for Awakening)*, 2013.

"entwined (the entanglement)" —epigraph: King Woman, "Entwined." *Celestial Blues*, Relapse Records, 2021, track 6.

"indigo tides" —epigraph: Bonnie x Clyde, "Indigo." *Indigo*, 2023.

"kiss of the wild" —epigraph: Florence & the Machine, "King." *Dance Fever*, Polydor Records, 2022, track 1.

"Like a River" —epigraph: Bishop Briggs, "River." *Church of Scars*, Teleport Records & Island Records, 2016, track 2.

"wolf den ((building a home))" —epigraph & italics as lyrics: LP, "Safe Here." *Churches*, SOTA/Dine Alone, 2021, track 12.

For more musical muses and inspirations, please find my Spotify playlist *MoonSpeak: Indigo Tides* (QR code below).

All art within these pages is in support of independent artists:

- ammonite, fern, & wild geranium tattoo design by Kerry Burke (Terra Vasa Tattoo, Philly)
- ammonite art: purchased on Etsy from NightingaleCraftery.
- botanical/mushroom/mystical sun art: purchased on Etsy from DesignsByMeganTurner.
- fern art: purchased on CreativeMarket from Anna Repp Illustration.

a final note

To anyone who has ever looked at their life and felt trapped, felt there must be something more... there is, and there can be.

Follow your intuition. You deserve better.

If you or someone you know is in need, please contact the domestic violence hotline (US: 800-799-7233), or the suicide hotline (in the US, call/text: 988).

You are not (& never will be) alone.

Don't give up.

...ammonite a constant reminder: *"live with the past, but don't dwell in it."* no matter how quickly or chaotically life seems to spiral out of control, there's always something beautiful to experience, witness, or behold.

about the poet

Tianna Godsey (she/they) writes by "night" and works for non-profit land conservation by day. Her poems and prose, including her debut collection *Singing through my Wolf Bones*, are largely inspired by the healing powers of the natural world and our human connection to nature and wildlife.

Follow her on IG @goldencracked_words or @embodiedhealingwithtianna. You can find more of her books and writing at creativetianna.com.

Thank you so much for reading this collection. If you enjoyed it, please consider leaving a thoughtful review. As an indie author, every review makes a difference. Your support means everything.